# Freshwater Biome

by Grace Hansen

Abdo
BIOMES
Kids

**abdopublishing.com**

Published by Abdo Kids, a division of ABDO, PO Box 398166, Minneapolis, Minnesota 55439.

Copyright © 2017 by Abdo Consulting Group, Inc. International copyrights reserved in all countries.
No part of this book may be reproduced in any form without written permission from the publisher.

Printed in the United States of America, North Mankato, Minnesota.

052016

092016

 THIS BOOK CONTAINS
RECYCLED MATERIALS

Photo Credits: AP Images, iStock, Shutterstock

Production Contributors: Teddy Borth, Jennie Forsberg, Grace Hansen

Design Contributors: Laura Mitchell, Dorothy Toth


Cataloging-in-Publication Data


Names: Hansen, Grace, author.

Title: Freshwater biome / by Grace Hansen.

Description: Minneapolis, MN : Abdo Kids, [2017] | Series: Biomes |
    Includes bibliographical references and index.

Identifiers: LCCN 2015959104 | ISBN 9781680805024 (lib. bdg.) |
    ISBN 9781680805581 (ebook) | ISBN 9781680806144 (Read-to-me ebook)

Subjects: LCSH: Freshwater ecology--Juvenile literature.

Classification: DDC 577.6--dc23

LC record available at http://lccn.loc.gov/2015959104

# Table of Contents

## What is a Biome?

A biome is a large area. Certain plants and animals live there. It also has a certain climate.

desert

forest

freshwater

marine

grassland

tundra

5

## Freshwater Biomes

Freshwater biomes are important to the Earth. Their water is made up of less than 1% salt. They are **sources** of drinking water.

Ponds and lakes are **standing** freshwater biomes. Some are very small. Others are huge. Lake Superior covers 31,000 square miles (80,000 km$^2$)!

9

Ponds and lakes are all over the world. Water temperatures vary. Some lakes are warm or cold all year. Some places have seasons. So water temperatures change year round.

11

Rivers and streams are flowing freshwater biomes. They flow in one direction.

13

The water is clear at the source. Lots of plants and animals live near the middle. The water picks up lots of stuff as it flows. So, water is murky at the river's mouth.

15

## Plants

Plants are important parts of freshwater biomes. They are habitats and food for animals. Plants also make **oxygen**.

17

Certain plants **thrive** in freshwater biomes. Water lilies float in water. They have large, flat leaves that soak up sunlight. Their stems can be 7 feet (2 m) long.

19

## Animals

Certain animals **thrive** in freshwater, too. River otters are great swimmers. They have webbed toes. Their hair is waterproof. They have lots of fat to keep them warm.

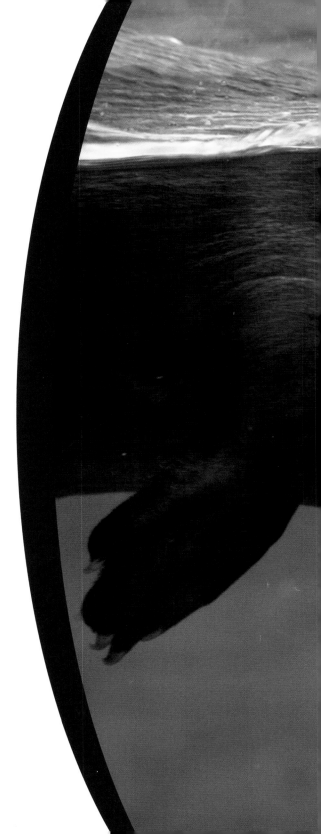

21

# Things You Might See in a Freshwater Biome

## animals

beaver

dragonfly

duck

## plants

bulrush

cattails

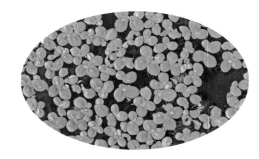

duckweed

22

# Glossary

climate – weather conditions that are usual in an area over a long period of time.

mouth – the place where a river enters the ocean.

murky – very dark or foggy.

oxygen – a chemical that is found in the air and is necessary for life.

source – the point of origin of a stream of water.

standing – not flowing.

thrive – to flourish or succeed.

# Index

# abdokids.com

Use this code to log on to abdokids.com and access crafts, games, videos, and more!

Abdo Kids Code:
BFK5024